PRAYING
GOD'S
WORD

DEVOTIONAL
JOURNAL

PRAYING
GOD'S
WORD

DEVOTIONAL
JOURNAL

BETH
MOORE

Nashville, Tennessee

PRAYING GOD'S WORD DEVOTIONAL JOURNAL
Copyright © 2002
Beth Moore
All Rights Reserved

Broadman & Holman Publishers
Nashville, Tennessee

Printed in Belgium
ISBN 10: 0-8054-3790-8
ISBN 13: 978-0-8054-3790-4

Edited by Dale McCleskey

Cover Photo: Photonica/Patrick Clark

7 8 9 10 11 12 13   10 09 08 07 06

DEDICATION

To my sister Gay,

You have always been there for me—
rain or shine, through thick and thin,
I can always count on you.
May we both continue to witness
the freedom of captives.
Christ is life, isn't He?

I love you,
Beth

INTRODUCTION

Sometimes we bow our heads to pray and no words come out. Perhaps that's because we've said the same words so often, we hesitate to re-use them into ritual. Or maybe it's because the day is so hard, the pain is so bad, words are somehow inadequate to express our hearts. Or maybe it's because we're pulled in so many different directions, we sometimes have trouble just stringing together a complete thought.

For any and all of these reasons, *Scripture prayers offer a refreshing source of clarity and purpose to our prayer lives.* They speak with the truth of the ages. They remain real and relevant in any situation. They resonate with the perfect will of God. And they put words in our mouth that remind us who we are in Christ—and Who this is we're speaking to as we pray.

This devotional journal has been designed to help you invite God's Word into your prayer times, letting His wisdom and eternal perspective keep your conversation anchored in the truth of His character. Oh, Satan can deceive us into believing so many lies. He can use our human nature against us to turn our thoughts inward and twist our understanding of what we see. But when the glowing light of God's Word is alive in our prayer life, His unchanging love, His total forgiveness, His tender hand, and His big-picture guidance can cut through the distortions and leave us standing in the warmth of true peace and hope.

None of these devotionals are dated, so you'll never get that "I'm behind, I've got to catch up" feeling. Perhaps you'll want to use the journaling space to react to these devotional thoughts and make connections between their messages and what's going on in your life. Perhaps you'll let the prayer starters lead you to write your own prayers as you lift them to the Father. Or perhaps you'll want to find other Bible passages that relate to these and record them here as a standing reference to come back to in facing life's challenges or in helping others deal with theirs. Mainly, we hope this book will minister to your heart and help you enjoy meaningful relationship with your Father.

GOD IS GREAT, GOD IS GOOD

The heavens praise your wonders, O LORD, your faithfulness too, in the assembly of the holy ones. For who in the skies above can compare with the LORD? Who is like the LORD among the heavenly beings?

—Psalm 89:5-6

IN YOUR OWN WORDS

Virtually every stronghold involves the worship of some kind of idol. For instance, the stronghold of pride is associated with the worship of self. The stronghold of addiction is associated with the worship of some kind of substance or habit. In one way or another, something else has become "god" in our lives, the object of our chief focus.

Filling our minds with Scriptures that acknowledge the "Godship" of God is a crucial part of renewing our lives and breaking our strongholds. Until we turn from our idols to the one true God, we will never find liberty. One missing link in almost every captive life is the spirit of God's lordship.

Liberty lives where God reigns as King.

O Lord my God, You are very great; You are clothed with splendor and majesty. You wrap Yourself in light as with a garment; You stretch out the heavens like a tent and lay the beams of Your upper chambers on their waters. You make the clouds Your chariot and ride on the wings of the wind. You make the winds Your messengers, flames of fire Your servants (Psalm 104:1-4). How great You are, God—beyond our understanding! (Job 36:26).

Lord, You have been our dwelling place throughout all generations. Before the mountains were born or You brought forth the earth and the world, from everlasting to everlasting You are God (Psalm 90:1-2).

HELP MY UNBELIEF

"If you can do anything, take pity on us and help us."
" 'If you can'?" said Jesus. "Everything is possible for him who
believes." Immediately the boy's father exclaimed, "I do believe; help
me overcome my unbelief!"   —Mark 9:22-24

IN YOUR OWN WORDS

Believing God is never more critical—nor more challenging—than when we are suffering under strongholds that need to be demolished. Why? Because we've battled most of our strongholds for years and tried countless remedies—with very little success—in an effort to be free.

The enemy taunts us with whispers like, *You'll never be free. You've tried a hundred times and you always go back. You're hopeless. You're weak. You're a failure. You don't have what it takes.* Every one of those statements about you is a lie if you are a believer in Christ, because you have Jesus—the Way, the Truth, and the Life. Believe He can do what He says He can do.

> *You can't just believe **in** Him*
> *to be free from your stronghold.*
> *You must **believe** Him.*

Father, please help me not to be like the ancient Israelites who willfully put You to the test (Psalm 78:18). They did not believe in You or trust in Your deliverance even after all the wonders You had shown them (Psalm 78:22). According to Your Word, it is possible to be broken off from part of Your plan because of unbelief (Romans 11:20). O Father, I don't want to miss any part of Your plan because of my own unbelief! Please forgive me for any unbelief, and help me walk by faith.

Father, according to Your Word, without faith it is impossible to please You, because anyone who comes to You must believe that You exist and that You reward those who earnestly seek You (Hebrews 11:6). Lord, I want to please You. Build faith in me so my life will honor the life of Your Son.

COUNTING OUR LIVES TOO DEAR

To fear the LORD *is to hate evil; I hate pride and arrogance, evil behavior and perverse speech.*

—*Proverbs 8:13*

Perhaps no other spiritual obstacle is quite like pride. The challenge to overcome pride may be the only common denominator on every one of our spiritual "to do" lists—for a simple reason. Pride is Satan's specialty. It is the characteristic that most aptly describes him. Pride is the issue that forced him to be expelled from heaven, and it is still one of his most successful tools in discouraging people from accepting the gospel of Jesus Christ.

Let's not fool ourselves into thinking that pride is a problem only for the lost. The most effective means the enemy uses to keep believers from being full of the Spirit is to keep us full of ourselves.

Pride is an enemy we all know—all too well. And all for nothing.

Father, Your Word says, "Before his downfall a man's heart is proud, but humility comes before honor" (Proverbs 18:12). I want to be a person of honor in Your sight, O God. Help me to clothe myself with humility toward others, because You oppose the proud but give grace to the humble (1 Peter 5:5). I will never live a day that I am not in need of Your grace, so please help me maintain an attitude that welcomes it.

Sovereign Lord, Your Word says, "This is the one I esteem: he who is humble and contrite in spirit, and trembles at my word" (Isaiah 66:2). Father, I can hardly imagine being someone You esteem, but I sincerely want to be! Make me that kind of person through the power of Your Holy Spirit.

THE LIES WE BELIEVE

Everyone lies to his neighbor;
their flattering lips speak with deception.

—Psalm 12:2

IN YOUR OWN WORDS

Nothing is bigger or more powerful than God; therefore, when anything other than Jesus Christ masters the Christian's life, that master can keep its grip only through pretension and deception.

Remember, Satan is the father of lies (John 8:44). No truth is in him. However, his specialty is in twisting a lie until it seems true. He sells us lies like . . . This isn't doing me any harm. I can handle it. I'll know just when to stop. After all the things I've been through, I deserve this.

The list of lies we often believe when we are held in a stronghold can be unlimited. But God's Word provides the truth that can override the onslaught of the devil's distortions.

Sin is a deception. That's what makes daily doses of truth so important.

Father God, You have adamantly warned Your children not to be deceived (James 1:16). Am I presently being deceived in any way? If I am, please reveal it to me, and give me the courage to cease cooperating with deceptive schemes. When I sin against You, Father, and choose to walk in deception rather than truth, please send others to gently instruct and confront me. Grant me repentance leading me to a knowledge of the truth (2 Timothy 2:25).

Lord God, I was once darkness, but now I am light in You. Help me to live now as a child of light, for the fruit of the light consists in all goodness, righteousness, and truth. Help me to seek You and find out what pleases You (Ephesians 5:8–10).

THE FEAR OF BEING UNLOVED

Though my father and mother forsake me, the LORD will receive me.

—Psalm 27:10

IN YOUR OWN WORDS

All of us have insecurities . . . even the most outwardly confident people we know.

Minor insecurities can be little more than occasional challenges, but when life suddenly erupts like a volcano, insecurity can turn into panic. *Want* suddenly feels like *need*. A hidden pocket of unmet needs suddenly quakes and leaves a cavern.

The fear or the feeling of being unloved is probably our greatest source of insecurity, whether or not we can always articulate it. But in Christ we have been adopted by grace into the eternal embrace of acceptance. Others can make us feel insecure in their love, but the Father loves us completely and unequivocally.

Let every twinge of insecurity remind you how secure you are in the Father.

Father, as surely as You convinced the apostle Paul, convince me thoroughly that neither death nor life, neither angels nor demons, neither the present nor the future, nor any powers, neither height nor depth, nor anything else in all creation, will be able to separate me from the love of God that is in Christ Jesus my Lord (Romans 8:38–39).

Lord God, show the wonder of Your great love, You who save by Your right hand those who take refuge in You from their foes. Keep me as the apple of Your eye; hide me in the shadow of Your wings (Psalm 17:7–8).

OVERCOMING REJECTION

Do not conform any longer to the pattern of this world, but be trans-formed by the renewing of your mind. Then you will be able to test and approve what God's will is—his good, pleasing, and perfect will.
—Romans 12:2

IN YOUR OWN WORDS

Rejection in and of itself is not a stronghold. It is our *reaction* to rejection that determines whether we become bound by it.

Only God knows the tragic number of His children who have allowed themselves to be imprisoned for the rest of their lives by continu-ing to harbor feelings of rejection. I would never imply that getting over rejection is easy, but overcoming it is possible for every person who puts his or her heart and mind to it. You over-come rejection by daily applying large doses of God's love to your wounded heart and by allow-ing Him to renew your mind until you learn to think like one who is accepted.

> *Overcoming rejection is God's unquestionable will for your life if you belong to Him.*

Lord God, I revel in Your promise that You will go before me and make the rough places smooth; You will shatter the doors of bronze and cut through their iron bars. And You will give me the treasures of darkness and hidden wealth of secret places, in order that I may know that it is You, the Lord, the God of Israel, who calls me by my name (Isaiah 45:2–3, NASB).

For the sake of Your great name, Lord, You will not reject Your people, because You, Lord, were pleased to make me Your own (1 Samuel 12:22). Praise your wonderful name!

MUCH TO TEACH

Everything that was written in the past was written to teach us, so that through endurance and the encouragement of the Scriptures we might have hope.

—*Romans 15:4*

IN YOUR OWN WORDS

Perhaps one of your strongholds is an addiction to a certain substance or behavior. Hear me: God can set you free. But what He requires from you is time, trust, and cooperation. The immense power of an addiction is rarely broken in a day.

You see, God has as much desire to *teach* us as to *overwhelm* us. He could show us His power by instantaneously setting us free from all desire for our stronghold. But few things beyond our salvation are "once and for all." If He delivered us instantly, we would see His greatness once, but we would soon forget. We'd risk going back.

On the other hand, if God teaches us victory in Christ Jesus day by day, we live in the constant awareness of His greatness and sufficiency.

> *God's usual healing method is the daily process of teaching us to walk with Him.*

Father, sometimes I feel like there is so much rubble, I can't rebuild the wall (Nehemiah 4:10). But Your Word claims that You are the Repairer of Broken Walls, and the Restorer of Streets with Dwellings (Isaiah 58:12). Please introduce Yourself to me by these wonderful names, and rebuild the rubble in my life. Cause my soul to yearn for You in the night and long for You in the morning (Isaiah 26:9).

Lord, Your Word says that he who trusts in himself is a fool, but he who walks in wisdom is kept safe (Proverbs 28:26). I've come to realize that I cannot trust in myself. My safety is in learning to trust in You. Please help me!

Lord of All

May God himself, the God of peace, sanctify you through and through.
May your whole spirit, soul, and body be kept blameless at the coming
of our Lord Jesus Christ. The one who calls you is faithful and he
will do it.　　　　　　　　　　　　*—1 Thessalonians 5:23-24*

In Your Own Words

What a relief to know we'll never battle anything out of God's jurisdiction. God can as easily defeat His opposition on Mt. Carmel as He can on Mt. Zion. It's all His turf.

The same is true in regard to our own battlegrounds. God created us to be whole creatures made of three different components: body, soul, and spirit. As long as we see God as Lord of our spirits alone, we will continue to live in areas of defeat. But God is as surely Lord of our souls and body as He is of our spirits. *It's all His turf.*

God Himself is at work in you and through you—at work in your body, at work in your personality and emotions. He is thoroughly interested and involved in every single part of you.

Nothing in your life is beyond God's ability to do something about it.

Lord, my enemy the devil prowls around like a roaring lion looking for someone to devour (1 Peter 5:8). But I find encouragement in knowing that many believers, weak in their natural selves, have walked faithfully and victoriously with You (Hebrews 11). Therefore, since I am surrounded by such a great cloud of witnesses, help me throw off everything that hinders and the sin that so easily entangles, and help me run with perseverance the race marked out for me (Hebrews 12:1).

O Lord, like David, help me to rejoice in Your strength and say of You, "How great is [my] joy in the victories you give!" Father, please grant me the desire of my heart to be free from this stronghold, and do not withhold the request of my lips (Psalm 21:1–2). Through the victories You give, may Christ's glory be great! (Psalm 21:5).

AUTHORITY TO FORGIVE

"That you may know that the Son of Man has authority on earth to forgive sins. . . ." He said to the paralyzed man, "I tell you, get up, take your mat and go home."

—Luke 5:24

IN YOUR OWN WORDS

In Luke 5:24, Christ announced emphatically, "The Son of Man has authority on earth to forgive sins." Indeed, the acceptance of God's forgiveness through Jesus Christ swings our prison doors wide open.

Satan knows that what Jesus "opens no one can shut, and what he shuts no one can open" (Revelation 3:7). If the devil is powerless to shut the prison doors which Christ has opened, then what is his next best option? He can work like crazy to convince us to stay, even though we're fully free, fully within our rights to leave. He can continue to wield the weapon of accusation, but we are not bound to listen to him. We only stay pinned in our prison cells by our own decision.

You are free to leave the past. And free to play dead to the devil.

Father, You have promised that those who sow in tears will reap with songs of joy. Those who go out weeping, carrying seed to sow, will return with songs of joy, carrying sheaves with them (Psalm 126:5–6). Lord, I have come with weeping: I have prayed as You brought me back. You will lead me beside streams of water on a level path where I will not stumble, because You are my Father (Jeremiah 31:9).

_____

_____

_____

_____

_____

_____

_____

_____

_____

_____

_____

_____

_____

_____

_____

_____

_____

Wash me, Lord, and I will be whiter than snow. Let me hear joy and gladness; let the bones You have crushed rejoice! (Psalm 51:7–8). Break this bondage, Lord, that seems to keep me from sensing or believing Your forgiveness. Help me to rejoice that the only thing whiter than snow is a repentant sinner!

THE ULTIMATE HEALER

O LORD my God, I called to you for help, and you healed me.
—Psalm 30:2

IN YOUR OWN WORDS

I believe I can confidently but reverently say to you that God can put any broken person back together again no matter what he or she has suffered. I'm not just saying that God can cause a person to maintain his or her physical existence after tragedy. He can truly help you *live* again.

I'll never forget my mother-in-law's response when I asked her how she survived the death of her beloved, blonde-headed 3-year-old after a house fire. She answered, "I just kept waking up. I didn't want to live. I simply didn't have much choice."

My heart still breaks for her, but I can tell you that she is no longer simply breathing. She is living once again. That's what God can do.

> *God can restore abundant life to anyone, in any situation.*

God, You are my refuge and strength, an ever-present help in trouble. Therefore I will not fear, though the earth give way and the mountains fall into the heart of the sea, though its waters roar and foam and the mountains quake with their surging (Psalm 46:1-3). I will be still and know You are God. You, Lord Almighty, are with me. You, God of Jacob, are my fortress (Psalm 46:10-11).

Lord, whom have I in heaven but You? And earth has nothing I desire besides You. My flesh and my heart may fail, but You, God, are the strength of my heart and my portion forever (Psalm 73:25-26).

EVERY BELIEVER'S TASK

"When you stand praying, if you hold anything against anyone,
forgive him, so that your Father in heaven may forgive you your sins."
                                                            —Mark 11:25

IN YOUR OWN WORDS

Strongholds present us with many challenges. Not all of them are the same for me as they are for you. But no matter how different the rest of our challenges may be, every believer can count on dealing with this one challenge: *to forgive*.

Remember, God's primary agenda in the life of a believer is to conform the child into the likeness of Jesus Christ. And no other word quite sums up His character in relationship to us like the word *forgiving*.

We never look more like Christ than when we forgive someone who has hurt us. And since that is God's goal for us, we're destined for plenty of opportunities!

Forgiveness takes more strength
than you have. It takes His.

Lord Jesus, when You were being led out to be executed, after being beaten, ridiculed, and spit upon, You said, "Father, forgive them, for they do not know what they are doing" (Luke 23:34). If You can forgive those kinds of things—being totally innocent—I can forgive the things that have been done to me. I also acknowledge that people who hurt me haven't always known what they were doing or what repercussions their actions would have.

Lord, I want it to be said of me that my many sins have been forgiven—for I have loved much (Luke 7:47). You have forgiven me for so much, Lord. Make it evident in the way I love You and love others.

AND AGAIN I SAY, FORGIVE

Peter came to Jesus and asked, "Lord, how many times shall I forgive my brother when he sins against me? Up to seven times?" Jesus answered, "I tell you, not seven times, but seventy-seven times."
—*Matthew 18:21-22*

IN YOUR OWN WORDS

We can safely say that we as ambassadors of Christ in this generation have literally been called to a ministry of forgiveness. So . . . how is your ministry going? Have you had lots of ups and downs? A few successes and a few too many failures?

Me too!

But I pray that God has been as unrelenting in His insistence upon your willingness to forgive as He has mine. The longer I've walked with God in prayer and His Word, and the more I've come to love Him, the less I've wanted for Him to let me off easy. I'm learning that a believer's willingness to do the hard thing is what sets him or her apart for the extraordinary in Christ.

Be glad God insists on expecting much from you.

Father God, if I love those who love me, what reward will I get? Are not even the godless doing that? And if I greet only those to whom I am close, what am I doing more than others? Do not even pagans do that? (Matthew 5:46–47). You have called me to be different, Lord—to go far beyond the actions of even the noblest pagan.

_____

_____

_____

_____

_____

_____

_____

_____

_____

_____

_____

_____

_____

_____

_____

_____

_____

_____

Lord, as hard as this may be for me to comprehend or rationalize, Your Word is clear: if I forgive others when they sin against me, You, my heavenly Father, will also forgive me (Matthew 6:14).

CHRISTLIKENESS IS THE GOAL

Those God foreknew he also predestined to be conformed to the likeness of his Son, that he might be the firstborn among many brothers.

—Romans 8:29

Satan does a masterful job of shaming those caught in strongholds into a continuous cycle of defeat. He cannot take our salvation away from us, so he does everything he can do in order to steal, kill, and destroy our character, testimony, and effectiveness.

One way he's doing this in our generation is in the area of sexual strongholds. Satan's attacks on sexuality have become so outright and blatant that we're becoming frighteningly desensitized to it all. Instead of measuring our lives against the goal of Christlikeness, we are beginning to subconsciously measure our lives against the world's depravity. We must be constantly on guard to keep God's purity our only standard.

There is a pleasure found in purity that no worldly pleasure can give.

Lord God, I do not understand what I do. For what I want to do I do not do, but what I hate I do (Romans 7:15). So I find this law at work: when I want to do good, evil is right there with me (Romans 7:21). And I hate it, Lord. I really do. For I know that I belong to the truth. This is how I set my heart at rest in Your presence whenever my heart condemns me. For You, God, are greater than my heart and You know everything (1 John 3:19-20).

Father, if I remain stubborn and unrepentant in heart, Your Word says I am storing up wrath for myself for the day of Your wrath (Romans 2:5). But by Your grace, I am able to store up glory, honor, and peace by doing good (Romans 2:10). I do not have to settle for a life hopelessly entangled in sin.

THE BATTLE RAGES

"Woe to the earth and the sea, because the devil has gone down to you! He is filled with fury, because he knows that his time is short."
—Revelation 12:12

IN YOUR OWN WORDS

Tragically, Satan has successfully duped the vast majority of our churches into imbalance regarding all things concerning or threatening him. We tend to give the devil either far too much credit or not nearly enough.

I cannot say this strongly enough: it is imperative in these days in which we've been assigned to occupy this earth that believers walk in truth and soundness of doctrine.

A war of unprecedented proportions is raging against the church and the people of God. We must put on our armor, learn how to use our weapons, and fight with the confidence of those who know they are destined to win.

> *You—yes, you!—can become a powerful foe of hell.*

Who is like Your children, O God, a people saved by the Lord? You are my shield and helper and my glorious sword. Cause my enemy to cower, Lord! Trample down his high places (Deuteronomy 33:29). Help me to be strong in You and in Your mighty power. Help me to put on Your full armor that I can take my stand against the devil's schemes (Ephesians 6:10-11), that I may be able to stand my ground, and after I have done everything, to stand (Ephesians 6:13).

Lord, when Your children, the Israelites, were defeated in a battle, You revealed to them that they were hanging on to something that did not belong to them. You said, "You cannot stand against your enemies until you remove it" (Joshua 7:13). I earnestly ask You to reveal anything in my life that could be hindering victory.

REHEARSING YOUR LINES

"These commandments that I give you today are to be upon your hearts. Impress them on your children. Talk about them when you sit at home and when you walk along the road, when you lie down and when you get up." —Deuteronomy 6:6–7

IN YOUR OWN WORDS

We often invest a lot more time focusing on our strongholds than on our Strong Deliverer. And as long as our minds rehearse the strength of our stronghold more than the strength of our God, we will always be impotent.

But as we pray the Word of God, acknowledging His limitless strength and transcendent dominion, Truth will begin to eclipse the lies. We will realize that in our weakness He is strong, that as we bend the knee to His Lordship, God is more than able to deliver us.

No matter how often you are tempted to review your problems, make sure that you review God's power more frequently.

You'll never see your way through unless you're focused on the Father.

My Father, if it were Your intention to withdraw Your Spirit and breath, all mankind would perish together and man would return to the dust (Job 34:14-15). Instead, my Lord, You have promised that Your plans for Your people are plans to prosper and not to harm, plans to give us hope and a future (Jeremiah 29:11). So instead of submitting to sin, I desire to love You, listen to Your voice, and hold fast to You—for You, Lord, are my life (Deuteronomy 30:20).

Yours, Lord, is the greatness and the power and the glory and the majesty and the splendor; for everything in heaven and earth is Yours. Yours, my own heavenly Father, is the kingdom, and You are exalted as head above all (1 Chronicles 29:11).

HAND-PICKED

"You did not choose me, but I chose you and appointed you to go and bear fruit—fruit that will last. Then the Father will give you whatever you ask in my name."

—*John 15:16*

IN YOUR OWN WORDS

You and I as believers in Christ have been chosen—*chosen!*—to know, believe, and understand that He is the one true God.

Think of it all! Heaven is His throne. Earth is His footstool. Awesome creatures never cease day or night singing, "Holy, Holy, Holy, Lord God Almighty!" Lightning flashes from His throne. The winds do His bidding. The clouds are His chariot. The earth trembles at the sound of His voice. When He stands to His feet, His enemies are scattered.

He is God and there is no other. Yet this very One is also our Father, who demands and deserves our respect. We are His by His good pleasure, and He is great by His own nature.

Your status before God is no accident, for He has chosen you.

Father God, Your Word declares that we, Your people, are Your witnesses and Your servants whom You have chosen, that we may know and *believe* You and understand that You are He. Before You no god was formed, nor will there be one after You (Isaiah 43:10). You have chosen me, God, for the express purpose of knowing and believing You. I can't really begin to know You until I choose to believe You! Make me a person of belief, Lord.

Lord God, I acknowledge that it is by grace I have been saved, through faith—and this not from myself; it is the gift of God (Ephesians 2:8).

LIKE IT OR LUMP IT

*"I will remove from this city those who rejoice in their pride.
Never again will you be haughty on my holy hill."*

—Zephaniah 3:11

IN YOUR OWN WORDS

Pride is one of our greatest enemies. No wonder the Bible states and restates that God hates it. Scripture exhorts believers, "Humble yourselves, therefore, under God's mighty hand" (1 Peter 5:6). The Word also makes this very unsettling statement in Daniel 4:37: "Those who walk in pride he is able to humble."

I believe the sum total of these two verses is this: either we can humble *ourselves*, or God can humble us *Himself.* God won't put up with pride in His own children very long without dealing with it. And one thing I know from personal experience is this: humbling ourselves is far less painful than inviting God to humble us, because He tends to make sure His lessons "take."

Let God deal with your pride before you're forced to deal with its consequences.

Father, according to Your Word, in his pride the wicked does not seek You; in all his thoughts there is no room for You (Psalm 10:4). But Lord, a time is certainly coming when the arrogance of man will be brought low and the pride of men humbled; You alone will be exalted in that day (Isaiah 2:17). Teach me to walk humbly with you. Don't allow me to continue on in pride that stops me from seeking You.

_____

_____

_____

_____

_____

_____

_____

_____

_____

_____

_____

_____

_____

_____

_____

_____

_____

_____

Lord, You instruct Your people to listen carefully and heed Your instruction because pride can cause the Lord's flock to be taken captive (Jeremiah 13:17). I pray that you would not only keep me from captivity but use me to lead others to freedom in You.

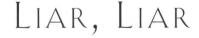

LIAR, LIAR

We have renounced secret and shameful ways; we do not use deception, nor do we distort the word of God. On the contrary, by setting forth the truth plainly we commend ourselves to every man's conscience in the sight of God.   —2 Corinthians 4:2

IN YOUR OWN WORDS

Sometimes we're very aware of tolerating or even fueling a lie. At other times we are caught in such a web that we can no longer see ourselves or our situations accurately. It's not always clear when we're being deceived. But one sure sign of it is this: when we ourselves begin to deceive.

All you have to do to locate Satan in any situation is to look for the lie. How do you recognize one? Anything you are believing or acting on that is contrary to what the truth of God's Word says about you is a lie. Today's passage helps us spot four of Satan's specialties—secrecy, shame, deception, and distortion of Scripture. Each of these spiritual crimes must be renounced and rejected in order for us to walk in victory.

Not sure whether a thought or idea is coming from Satan? Just follow the lies.

Lord God, just as Eve was deceived by the serpent's cunning, the minds of even those with a sincere and pure devotion to Christ can be led astray (2 Corinthians 11:3). O Merciful Father, please help me never to exchange the truth of God for a lie (Romans 1:25). If any area remains in my life where I have made such a tragic exchange, reveal it and set me free.

Lord, surely You desire truth in my inner parts; You teach me wisdom in the inmost place (Psalm 51:6). Please expose to me the deeply embedded lies I've believed, and replace them with permanently engraved truth.

WHAT I REALLY NEED

What a man desires is unfailing love; better to be poor than a liar.
—Proverbs 19:22

Jehovah God, the Great Soul-ologist, identified man's chief desire in today's verse. More than anything, we want His "unfailing love."

But what in the world does being better off "poor than a liar" have to do with a man's desiring this "unfailing love"?

Think about it for a moment! The Holy Spirit is pinpointing the deep origin of our constant cravings to have more and more of *any*thing. He is implying that our human tendency to stockpile belongings or amass wealth is a clear indication of a cavernous need in our souls. What we need—every one of us—is not some kind of financial security but the loyal love of a faithful heavenly Father.

All we really need is something we already have: God's unfailing love.

Lord, You cover me with Your feathers and grant me refuge under Your wings; Your faithfulness will be my shield and rampart. I need not fear the terror of night, nor the arrow that flies by day, nor the pestilence that stalks in the darkness, nor the plague that destroys at midday (Psalm 91:4-6). For though the mountains be shaken and the hills be removed, yet Your unfailing love for me will not be shaken nor Your covenant of peace be removed (Isaiah 54:10).

Lord, many are the woes of the wicked, but Your unfailing love surrounds the one who trusts in You (Psalm 32:10). You are so trustworthy, God. Please help me to place my complete trust in You.

No Rejects

"May the LORD our God be with us as he was with our fathers; may he never leave us nor forsake us."

—1 Kings 8:57

Jesus Christ will never leave you or forsake you.

• He will never cast you away.

• He will never lose the last ounce of His long patience and decide He doesn't want you as a member of His family any more.

• If you have received Christ as your Savior, nothing you can do will cause Him to reject you.

Believe all these things that God's Word tells you about Him, and believe all the things His Word tells you about *you*. You are defined by the love and acceptance of the Creator and Sustainer of the universe. He happens to think you are worth loving—and keeping. Find the full measure of your identity in Him and in Him alone.

> *Read the Bible and see for yourself: you are very important to God.*

Jesus, through You we have access to the Father by one Spirit. Consequently, we are no longer foreigners and aliens, but fellow citizens with God's people and members of God's household, built on the foundation of the apostles and prophets, with You Yourself as the chief cornerstone. In You the whole building is joined together and rises to become a holy temple in the Lord. And in You, we are being built together to become a dwelling in which God lives by His Spirit (Ephesians 2:18-22).

Lord God, You pose the question in Your Word, "Can a mother forget the baby at her breast and have no compassion on the child she has borne?" You assure me that though she may forget, You will absolutely never forget me! You have engraved me on the palms of Your hands (Isaiah 49:15–16).

COMMON ENEMIES

What, then, shall we say in response to this? If God is for us, who can be against us?

—Romans 8:31

IN YOUR OWN WORDS

Begin to see yourself like the young shepherd boy, David, when he dared to take a stand against Goliath. David wasn't blind. He was realistically aware of the mammoth size of his foe. What was the key to his courage?

David knew that Goliath was not only *his* enemy; he was also *God's* enemy! When David saw the Philistine champion from Gath step out and shout "his usual defiance," he asked, "Who is this uncircumcised Philistine that he should defy the armies of the living God?" (1 Samuel 17:26). If you have a sin or addiction that continues to shout its defiance at all your attempts to fight it, realize that your enemy is also God's enemy. And He will conquer His opponents.

You're not fighting alone.
Your God is fighting for you.

O Lord, our God, other lords besides You have ruled over me, but Your name alone is the one I want to honor (Isaiah 26:13). Your Word says that when I offer myself to someone or something to obey as a slave, I am a slave to the one whom I obey, whether I am a slave of sin, which leads to death, or to obedience, which leads to righteousness (Romans 6:16). O Father, I deeply desire to be a slave only to You.

Father, I know that in all things You work for the good of those who love You, who have been called according to Your purpose (Romans 8:28). You can and will work my most terrible challenges for good if I will cooperate with You and see myself as one called according to Your purpose.

PEACE ON EARTH

Let the peace of Christ rule in your hearts, since as members of one body you were called to peace. And be thankful.

—Colossians 3:15

IN YOUR OWN WORDS

Scripture identifies God specifically as the "God of peace" (1 Thessalonians 5:23). The Word of God is perfectly inspired; therefore every identification of God, every name He is called, is in perfect context. In this case the inference of the title is that the believer will be awash with God's peace when every part of the life—body, soul, and spirit—is surrendered to His wise, loving, and liberating authority.

I know far too well how distant the peace of God is when we refuse to bow a part of our lives to His rule. Peace is the fruit of authority—God's authority. Let it reign and rule there. Let it stand above us. Christ always brings His peace where He is Prince.

Wherever Christ rules in your life, His peace will follow.

Father, the false teachers of this world promise freedom, while they themselves are slaves of depravity—for a man is a slave to whatever has mastered him (2 Peter 2:19). I acknowledge my slavery and deeply desire to be mastered by You alone. Only Your mastery brings liberty.

Lord, whatever is true, whatever is noble, whatever is right, whatever is pure, whatever is lovely, whatever is admirable—if anything is excellent or praiseworthy—help me to make the choice to think about such things (Philippians 4:8).

CASE CLOSED

He gives us more grace. That is why the Scripture says: "God opposes the proud but gives grace to the humble."

—James 4:6

Never in all of Scripture did Christ resist the repentant sinner. Indeed, forgiveness is why He came. So when we approach God in genuine repentance, taking full responsibility for our own sins, our prison doors swing open. Tragically, though, too many of us sit right there for years in our prison cells, living in the torment of guilt, feeling unreleased from repetitive sins.

Satan knows that forgiveness leads to freedom, so he takes on the role of tormentor, taunting us with guilt and condemnation. He does everything he can to see to it that we don't forgive ourselves. But we have God's promises that our penalty has been paid, our time served, our guilt expunged. We can walk forward in His truth.

Satan can scream and holler all he wants to. We're free to ignore him.

Father God, thank You for declaring no condemnation for those who are in Christ Jesus, because through Christ Jesus the law of the Spirit of life set me free from the law of sin and death (Romans 8:1-2). Help me to understand that the loving chastisement that might come to me after I have rebelled against You is only in the purest Father's love and is never to be confused with condemnation (Hebrews 12:6).

My faithful God, if I claim to be without sin, I deceive myself and the truth is not in me. But if I confess my sins, You are faithful and just and will forgive me my sins and purify me from all unrighteousness (1 John 1:8–9).

HOPE WHERE IT HURTS

"I grieve for you, Jonathan my brother; you were very dear to me. Your love for me was wonderful, more wonderful than that of women."
—2 Samuel 1:26

IN YOUR OWN WORDS

I approach the topic of loss with tenderness of heart, because those who have experienced loss truly know the meaning of the word *devastation*. Perhaps you are having to adjust to life without a precious loved one, and you find yourself in a season of ongoing despair or you're trying desperately to avoid one. Perhaps you are a dear friend of someone who is facing a time when the world has seemed to fall out of its orbit.

Grief is a normal, appropriate response to loss; it is most assuredly not a stronghold. But the burden of lengthy, life-draining despair definitely is. To block the healing, restorative power of God places a believer in a painful, debilitating yoke of bondage that we never have to go through.

People suffering from a loss need all the encouragement they can get.

Father, You inspired the Psalmist to confess, "It was good for me to be afflicted so that I might learn your decrees. The law from your mouth is more precious to me than thousands of pieces of silver and gold" (Psalm 119:71-72). We never know what You and Your Word can mean and do until we are so afflicted that we cannot live without You. Please grant me an abundance of You, and teach me Your powerful Word so that meaning can come forth from tragedy.

One thing I ask of You, Lord; this is what I seek: that I may dwell in the house of the Lord all the days of my life, to gaze upon Your beauty and to seek You in Your temple. For in the day of trouble You will keep me safe in Your dwelling; You will hide me in the shelter of Your tabernacle and set me high upon a rock (Psalm 27:4–5).

THE FREEDOM OF FORGIVENESS

As God's chosen people, holy and dearly loved, clothe yourselves with compassion, kindness, humility, gentleness and patience. Bear with each other and forgive whatever grievances you may have against one another. Forgive as the Lord forgave you.   —Colossians 3:12-13

IN YOUR OWN WORDS

Each of us has been confronted by some pretty overwhelming challenges to forgive. Some seem . . . well, unforgivable. For instance, sometimes the person who has hurt us isn't even sorry. Or won't take responsibility. Or is in the grave. Perhaps the person simply doesn't deserve our forgiveness. After all, forgiveness would make everything OK, and we want the record to show: we are *not* OK!

But if we let truth have its way, it will begin to eclipse our mound of excuses. We'll realize that we really won't be OK *until* we forgive. If only we could understand that God's unrelenting insistence on our forgiveness is not just for the sake of the one who hurt us, but for our own.

Forgiveness is in many ways a gift to ourselves.

Father, help me understand that the punishment and repercussions that come to people when they have done wrong is often sufficient for them. Instead of causing more grief, Your Word says I ought to forgive and comfort the person, so that he or she will not be overwhelmed by excessive sorrow (2 Corinthians 2:6-7). Help me to be the kind of person I'd want ministering to me after I had failed.

Lord, I do not want to be like those who refuse to pay attention to You. Please help me not to turn my back in stubbornness and stop up my ears just because Your will is hard at times. Help me not to make my heart as hard as flint and refuse to listen to the words that You, Lord Almighty, have sent by Your Spirit (Zechariah 7:11-12).

POISONOUS PLANTS

See to it that no one misses the grace of God and that no bitter root grows up to cause trouble and defile many.

—Hebrews 12:15

IN YOUR OWN WORDS

God is faithful. He will plead our case and take up our cause . . . but only when we make a deliberate decision to cease representing ourselves in the matter. And nowhere is that more true than in the area of forgiveness.

Innumerable strongholds are connected to an unwillingness to forgive. Left untreated, unforgiveness becomes spiritual cancer. Bitterness takes root. And since the root feeds the rest of the tree, every branch of our lives ultimately becomes diseased. The fruit on each limb becomes poisoned. Beloved sister or brother, the bottom line is: unforgiveness makes us sick. Spiritually. Emotionally. And surprisingly often, even physically. It is well worth getting over.

Forgiveness fixes a lot more problems than you think.

If You, O Lord, kept a record of sins, who could stand? But with You there is forgiveness; therefore You are feared (Psalm 130:3-4). After all You've done for me, Lord, after all the sin You've forgiven in my life, help me to have so much fear and reverence for You that I will not withhold forgiveness from others.

Lord, You have extended such grace to me. You have forgiven my wickedness and remembered my sins no more (Hebrews 8:12). Help me to demonstrate my heart of gratitude by forgiving others!

NOT ANY MORE

Do you not know that the wicked will not inherit the kingdom of God? . . . And that is what some of you were. But you were washed, you were sanctified, you were justified in the name of the Lord Jesus Christ and by the Spirit of our God.   —1 Corinthians 6:9,11

IN YOUR OWN WORDS

Satan's present employment of blatant sexual tactics is unparalleled in human history. He has never had the kind of universal audience which Internet access has accomplished for him. Now we can sit in our homes and open the attic door of pornography without paying even the price of embarassment. And since the rate of Christians being snared is so staggering, the church must start mentioning the unmentionable and biblically address issues attacking our generation.

God's Word applies to the strongholds of promiscuity, perversity, and pornography, just as it does to any other. God is not shocked. He has the remedy. He is merely awaiting our humble, earnest cry for help.

Want to hear something shocking? God can cure us of sexual sin.

Lord God, I acknowledge that my body was not meant for sexual immorality but for You, Lord. You were meant to take authority over this body and bring it sanctification and meaning. I know that my body is a member of Christ Himself. I shall not, then, take the members of Christ and unite them in an ungodly relationship (1 Corinthians 6:13–15).

_____

_____

_____

_____

_____

_____

_____

_____

_____

_____

_____

_____

_____

_____

_____

_____

_____

O Lord, You have searched me and You know me. You know when I sit and when I rise; You perceive my thoughts from afar. You discern my going out and my lying down; You are familiar with all my ways (Psalm 139:1–3). Help me to be completely truthful with You. I don't need to hide anymore.

IS YOUR GOD TOO SMALL?

Know that the LORD is God. It is he who made us, and we are his;
we are his people, the sheep of his pasture.

—Psalm 100:3

Our perception of God is often something that we ourselves have conjured up and does not represent the one true God at all. The truth may be that we've carved a "God" out of our own image, assigned Him the utmost and noblest of human characteristics, unintentionally envisioning Him to be more of a "superhuman" than the sovereign *El Elyon*—The Most High God.

I pray that you will develop a more accurate perception of God. I think sometimes He must listen to our pitifully small acclamations, expectations, and petitions in prayer, and want to say, "Are you talking to Me? I'm not recognizing Myself in this conversation. Are you sure you have the right God?"

> *We cannot settle for men's thoughts about God. We must know Him in His fullness.*

The earth is Yours, O Lord, and everything in it, the world and all who live in it (Psalm 24:1). For You, my Lord, are a great God, the great King above all gods. In Your hand are the depths of the earth, and the mountain peaks belong to You. The sea is Yours, for You made it, and Your hands formed the dry land (Psalm 95:3–5). Allow me to see You as You really are.

My mighty God, in Your hand is the life of every creature and the breath of all mankind (Job 12:10). You, my God, open Your hand and satisfy the desires of every living thing (Psalm 145:16).

ON EARTH AS IT IS IN HEAVEN

Jesus answered, "The work of God is this: to believe in the one he has sent."

—John 6:29

I am convinced that God would rather hear our honest pleas for more of what we lack than a host of pious platitudes from an unbelieving heart. When I am challenged with unbelief, I have begun to make this earnest plea to the One who will gladly supply: "Help my unbelief!"

Scripture prayers can fuel your faith in the One who is faithful and can fuel your belief in the One who is believable. It is always God's will for you to be free from strongholds. We may not always be sure God wills to heal us physically in this life of every disease or to prosper us with tangible blessings, but He always wills to free us from strongholds. "It is for freedom that Christ has set us free" (Galatians 5:1).

> *When you ask God to break a stronghold, you are always praying in the Father's will.*

Lord Jesus, according to Your Word, You are not bothered by our requests. Once when others told a synagogue leader not to bother You any more with his request, You ignored what they said and told the ruler, "Don't be afraid: just believe" (Mark 5:35–36). Help me not to be discouraged to pray and not to be afraid, but believe!

Lord, if You speak to me regarding earthly things and I do not believe, how then will I believe when You speak of heavenly things? (John 3:12). Help me to believe You here and now, not just in things concerning heaven. You are God of heaven *and* earth!

CUT US DOWN TO SIZE

When pride comes, then comes disgrace, but with humility comes wisdom.
—Proverbs 11:2

I am absolutely convinced that the most painful season God has taken me through to date was primarily to shatter my yoke of pride. It was a yoke, incidentally, that I didn't even recognize I had. Believe me, I'm on the lookout for it now every single day!

In some ways Christians have to be more alert to pride than anyone. If we don't presently have an issue that is actively humbling us, we veer with disturbing velocity toward arrogance and self-righteousness.

We are wise to remember that Christ never resisted the repentant sinner. Instead He resisted the religiously proud and Pharisaic.

> *Your greatest stumbling blocks show up on the road to self-centeredness.*

Lord, according to Your Word, after Uzziah became powerful, his pride led to his downfall. He was unfaithful to the Lord his God (2 Chronicles 26:16). The Israelites, too, were deceived by the pride of their hearts, and You brought them down from what they thought was a position of safety (Jeremiah 49:16). Help me understand that pride in my heart can deceive me, and never allow it to gain a foothold in my life.

God, I know that a man's pride brings him low, but a man of lowly spirit gains honor (Proverbs 29:23). Help me understand what You mean by a lowly or humble spirit. I want to be a person who gains honor in Your sight.

WIDE OPEN SPACES

"I have not spoken in secret, from somewhere in a land of darkness; I have not said to Jacob's descendants, 'Seek me in vain.' I, the LORD, speak the truth; I declare what is right."

—Isaiah 45:19

Satan's plans toward the believer are always the antithesis of God's.

Our Redeemer wants to loose us from the closets of secrecy and bring us into a spacious place of joy, freedom, authenticity, and transparency. Satan wants to keep us bound in secrecy where he can weigh us down in guilt, misery, and shame.

Oh, beloved, I know from experience that so much of the shame we experience in life is wrapped up in the secrets we keep. In fact, the enemy knows that once we expose the secret places of our lives to the light of God's Word, we're on our way to freedom. Are you ready to let the light shine into your darkness?

Life feels better and brighter when we live it out in the open.

Heavenly Father, this moment I am choosing the way of truth. I want to set my heart on Your laws (Psalm 119:30). I know Your love and truth always protect me (Psalm 40:11). Father, please help me learn how much Your truth protects me. Without it, I am vulnerable to the enemy and to my own flesh nature.

Father, Your Word exhorts us to buy the truth and never to sell it—to get wisdom, discipline, and understanding (Proverbs 23:23). Help me to understand that sometimes truth is costly but not nearly as costly as deception. Truth will never fail to return enormous dividends.

A LOVE BEYOND FEELINGS

"As the Father has loved me, so have I loved you.
Now remain in my love."

—John 15:9

IN YOUR OWN WORDS

Each of us craves utterly unfailing love—a love that is unconditional, unwavering, radical, demonstrative, broader than the horizon, deeper than the sea. And it would be nice if that love were healthy and whole, liberating rather than suffocating.

Interestingly, the Word of God uses the phrase "unfailing love" as many as 33 times, and not one of them refers to any source other than God Himself. You see, because God created us, He got to make us any way He wanted us. It's not His will for anyone to perish, and since the only way to have eternal life is to receive Him, God created us with a cavernous need that we would always need filling until we found Him.

If we have the love of God,
we have all we really need.

My faithful God, help me to call this to mind and therefore always have hope: because of Your great love, I am not consumed, for Your compassions never fail. They are new toward me every morning; great is Your faithfulness. I will say to myself, "The Lord is my portion; therefore, I will wait for him" (Lamentations 3:21-24). O God, help me to meditate on Your unfailing love! (Psalm 48:9).

Lord, thank You for showing Your love by sending Your one and only Son into the world that I might live through Him. This is love: not that I loved You, but that You loved me and sent Your Son as an atoning sacrifice for my sins (1 John 4:9-10).

YOU KNOW HOW IT FEELS?

He was in the world, and though the world was made through him, the world did not recognize him. He came to that which was his own, but his own did not receive him.

—John 1:10-11

The first suffering of Christ recorded in the Gospel of John is found in the eleventh verse of chapter 1: "He came to that which was his own, but his own did not receive him."

Rejection. Remember, these were Christ's own people. He loved them. His heart must have longed to be accepted by them. The Hebrew people shared a sense of community with which we have little to compare in our society. To be excluded from the fellowship and acceptance of that community was considered a fate worse than death by many.

Whatever rejection you face in your life, Jesus can understand. He has gone before us on the road of rejection.

Jesus can understand whatever rejection you face, for He has faced rejection too.

Dear Lord, why am I always surprised at the painful trials I suffer, as though something strange were happening to me? Help me to rejoice that I participate in the sufferings of Christ, so that I may be overjoyed when Your glory is revealed. If I am insulted because of the name of Your Son, I am blessed, for the Spirit of glory and of God rests on me (1 Peter 4:12–14).

Father God, I ask You to lead me when I'm blinded by ways I have not known. Along unfamiliar paths, please guide me. Lord, turn the darkness into light before me, and make the rough places smooth. I pray that these are the things You will do; I know You will not forsake me (Isaiah 42:16).

THE FIGHT OF OUR LIVES

I do not run like a man running aimlessly; I do not fight like a man beating the air. No, I beat my body and make it my slave so that after I have preached to others, I myself will not be disqualified for the prize.
—1 Corinthians 9:26-27

God could fight your toughest sins and addictions all alone. He really doesn't need your help. He reserves the right, however, to involve us in our own victories, so get ready to fight.

Overcoming these bitter curses may be the biggest battle of your life. But it will also be the most rewarding, liberating *victory* of your life. It will be your own Goliath story for the rest of your days.

So call upon God to rise up in anger toward the enemy that binds you, asking Him to fight on your behalf with a holy vengeance. Realize that God's unquestionable will is your freedom from this yoke, but also trust that He has written a personalized prescription for your release.

You may be in for a battle, but the Champion is in your corner.

God, according to Your Word, since Christ is in me, my body is dead because of sin, yet my spirit is alive because of righteousness. And if the Spirit of Him who raised Jesus from the dead is living in me, He who raised Christ from the dead will also give life to my mortal body through His Spirit, who lives in me (Romans 8:10-11).

I confess, Lord, that I am overwhelmed by the task ahead, but I am thankful that You have authority over all things. Heaven is Your throne and earth is Your footstool (Matthew 5:34-35); therefore, anything over my head is under Your feet!

THROUGH AND THROUGH

This is my prayer: that your love may abound more and more in knowledge and depth of insight, so that you may be able to discern what is best and may be pure and blameless until the day of Christ.
—*Philippians 1:9-10*

IN YOUR OWN WORDS

Don't miss what God desires to do in our lives. First Thessalonians 5:23 tells us that the glorious God of peace wants to sanctify us "through and through." The original Greek word for "sanctify" is *hagiazo*, meaning "to make clean, render pure, to consecrate, devote, set apart from a common to a sacred use, to regard and venerate as holy, to hallow." In other words, God deeply desires for us to grant Him total access to every single part of our lives—body, soul, and spirit. God's inclusion of the physical body is proof among many others in Scripture that He cares deeply what happens to these tents of flesh in which we dwell. Indeed, our physical bodies are the temples of the Holy Spirit (1 Corinthians 6:19).

God desires our all, but only that He may transform every part of us for His glory.

God, I do not consider myself yet to have taken hold of it. But one thing I do: forgetting what is behind and straining toward what is ahead, I press on toward the goal to win the prize for which You have called me heavenward in Christ Jesus (Philippians 3:13–14). Help me to forget all past failures—even past achievements—and focus now on pressing forward with You.

Lord, according to Your Word, everyone born of You overcomes the world. This is the victory that has overcome the world, even our faith. Who is it that overcomes the world? I do—when I truly believe that Jesus is the Son of God (1 John 5:4–5).

THE ACCUSER

I heard a loud voice in heaven say: "Now have come the salvation and the power and the kingdom of our God, and the authority of his Christ. For the accuser of our brothers, who accuses them before our God day and night, has been hurled down." —*Revelation 12:10*

IN YOUR OWN WORDS

Picture a death-row inmate in his cramped prison cell. Evidence of who he's been is scribbled all over the walls. Now picture the inmate receiving a pardon. Imagine the click of the key in the lock, the music of the hinges as they swing open.

But before the inmate can stand to his feet and walk out, the warden comes into the cell, sits beside him, and says, "You can't leave. You know what you've done. You know you're guilty as charged. You know you deserve this filthy, miserable cell. Read what is written all over these walls. That's the real you. You're a death-row inmate. You'll never be free. Just sit right here with me, and I'll keep you company." Does that sound like somebody's voice you know?

> *Satan says, "You'll never be free." Jesus says, "You're free already!"*

Father, my guilt has overwhelmed me like a burden too heavy to bear (Psalm 38:4). So I confess my iniquity; I am troubled by my sin. Many are my vigorous enemies; those who hate me without reason are numerous. Those who repay my good with evil slander me when I pursue what is good. O Lord, do not forsake me; be not far from me, O my God. My Savior, come quickly to help me (Psalm 38:18-22).

My faithful God, thank You for causing me to come to my senses and escape from the trap of the devil, who had taken me captive to do his will (2 Timothy 2:26).

JUST LET IT GO

He has rescued us from the dominion of darkness and brought us into the kingdom of the Son he loves, in whom we have redemption, the forgiveness of sins.

—Colossians 1:13-14

Forgiveness is not defined by a feeling, although it will ultimately change our feelings. The Greek word most often translated "forgiveness" in the New Testament is *aphiemi*, meaning "to send forth or away, to let go from oneself, from one's power or possession, from one's further attendance and occupancy."

Forgiveness is our deliberate willingness to let something go—not haphazardly into the black hole of nonexistence, but to let it go to *God*—to let it go from our power to His. Forgiveness is the ongoing act by which we agree with God over the matter, practice the mercy He's extended to us, and surrender the situation, the repercussions, and the hurtful person to Him.

A critical, unforgiving heart piles on one unnecessary load after another.

Father God, Your Word asks me why I judge or look down on my brother. I acknowledge to You today, Lord, that we will all stand before Your judgment seat (Romans 14:10). So then, each of us will give an account of himself to You. Therefore, help me stop passing judgment on others. Instead, I make up my mind not to put any stumbling block or obstacle in my brother's way (Romans 14:12–13).

Lord Jesus, how I can say to my brother, "Let me take the speck out of your eye," when all the time there is a plank in my own eye? Rescue me from being a hypocrite! Give me the honesty and courage to first take the plank out of my own eye, and then I may see clearly to remove the speck from my brother's eye (Matthew 7:4-5).

FADING TO BLACK

Why are you downcast, O my soul? Why so disturbed within me? Put your hope in God, for I will yet praise him, my Savior and my God.

—Psalm 42:5

Believers debate whether Christians can experience depression, but our ranks are nonetheless experiencing it in record numbers. What injury we bring to the hurting when we become both judge and jury, misapplying Scripture to the depth of another person's pain!

First John 1:6 says, "If we claim to have fellowship with him yet walk in darkness, we lie and do not live by the truth." But this verse has been wrongfully interpreted to mean that Christians do not experience seasons of darkness. Believers are most assuredly people of light, but sometimes the darkness around us can be so oppressive that we feel it. No, we are not *of* the darkness. But sometimes we *feel* the darkness.

There is light to be found in your deepest darkness.

God, You will give me the treasures of darkness, riches stored in secret places, so that I may know that You are the Lord, the God of Israel, who summons me by name (Isaiah 45:3). Lord, even in this difficult place, You have treasures for me here. You want me to discover the riches of relationship with You that will set me free.

Listen to my cry, Lord, for I am in desperate need; rescue me from those who pursue me, for they are too strong for me (Psalm 142:6). I am literally unable to be victorious without You. Come and rescue me with Your mighty hand.

KEEPING YOURSELF PURE

One of the seven angels who had the seven bowls full of the seven last plagues came and said to me, "Come, I will show you the bride, the wife of the Lamb."

—Revelation 21:9

IN YOUR OWN WORDS

One reason Satan has turned up the heat so furiously in temptations toward sexual sin in our generation is because he knows that the bride of Christ is supposed to be making herself ready for the Marriage Supper of the Lamb.

In 2 Corinthians 11:2–3, the apostle Paul expressed the heart of God in his desire that the church be presented as a "pure virgin" to Christ. Paul went on to say, "But I am afraid that just as Eve was deceived by the serpent's cunning, your minds may somehow be led astray from your sincere and pure devotion to Christ."

What better way than sexual temptation to tarnish people who are supposed to be presented as pure virgins to Christ?

You are pure before Christ.
But are you pure in heart today?

My merciful God, since I have been raised with Christ, set my heart on things above, where Christ is seated at the right hand of God. Help me set my mind on things above, not on earthly things (Colossians 3:1-2). Lord, please take my passions and redirect them first and foremost toward You. Be the chief focus of my life, and create a new heart within me with healthy emotions.

Christ Jesus, I count myself dead to sin but alive to God in You. Therefore I will not let sin reign in my mortal body so that I obey its evil desires. I choose not to offer the parts of my body to sin, as instruments of wickedness, but rather I offer myself to God, as one who has been brought from death to life. I offer the parts of my body to You as instruments of righteousness (Romans 6:11-13).

ALTERNATIVE SAVIORS

Your kingdom is an everlasting kingdom, and your dominion endures through all generations.

—Psalm 145:13

IN YOUR OWN WORDS

I will never forget the story I once heard about a Sunday school teacher who gave his elementary school class an assignment on Easter Sunday. He asked them each to make an acrostic of the word "E-A-S-T-E-R." He was stunned by one student's perception. The child had written: Every Alternative Savior Takes Early Retirement.

What a thought-provoking statement!

Hear this from a former captive: every alternative savior must take early retirement if we are ever to be free. Only one God can deliver us. The most monumental leap we take toward freedom is the leap to our knees—the lordship of Jesus Christ.

What alternative saviors need to be sent into early retirement in your life?

Lord, from one man You made every nation of men, that they should inhabit the whole earth; and You determined the times set for them and the exact places where they should live. You, my Father, did this so that men would seek You and perhaps reach out for You and find You, though You are not far from each one of us. For in You we live and move and have our being! (Acts 17:26-28).

_____

_____

_____

_____

_____

_____

_____

_____

_____

_____

_____

_____

_____

_____

_____

_____

_____

_____

_____

O Lord my God, many are the wonders You have done. The things You planned for us no one can recount to You. Were I to speak and tell of them, they would be too many to declare (Psalm 40:5).

FEEL THE POWER

In his great mercy he has given us new birth into a living hope through the resurrection of Jesus Christ from the dead . . . who through faith are shielded by God's power until the coming of the salvation that is ready to be revealed in the last time. —1 Peter 1:3,5

IN YOUR OWN WORDS

God wields incomparably great power for those who choose to believe—more than enough to break the yoke of any bondage! As believers we approach every circumstance of life as victors. No power, event, failure, person, place, or thing can defeat the immeasurable greatness of God's power in Christ!

"I pray also that the eyes of your heart may be enlightened in order that you may know the hope to which he has called you, the riches of his glorious inheritance in the saints, and *his incomparably great power for us who believe.* That power is like the working of his mighty strength, *which he exerted in Christ when he raised him from the dead*" (Ephesians 1:18–20, emphasis mine).

We can approach all of life with the absolute assurance of victory in Christ.

Christ Jesus, You said to Thomas, "Put your finger here; see my hands. Reach out your hand and put it into my side. Stop doubting and believe" (John 20:27). Lord, I cannot see Your visible hands, but if I'm willing to really look, I can see the visible evidences of Your invisible hands. Help me to stop doubting your power. Help me to believe!

Father, You have written Your Word to those who believe in the name of Your Son, so that we may know that we have eternal life (1 John 5:13). Help me to know and cease doubting.

PRIDE BY ANY OTHER NAME

By the grace given me I say to every one of you: Do not think of yourself more highly than you ought, but rather think of yourself with sober judgment, in accordance with the measure of faith God has given you.   *—Romans 12:3*

IN YOUR OWN WORDS

Remember, pride wears many masks. I once spoke on pride only to have someone remark afterward that she had far too little self-esteem to have pride.

But pride is not the opposite of low self-esteem. Pride is the opposite of *humility*. We can have a serious pride problem that masquerades as low self-esteem. Pride is self-absorption that exists whether we're absorbed with how miserable we are or how wonderful we are. Either condition can fall victim to hideous pride.

We are wise to be on the constant lookout for pride in our lives. We can safely say that if we're not deliberately taking measures to combat it, we're probably doing things to combat humility.

> *The humble don't think any less of themselves; they simply spend less time on themselves.*

Lord God, Your Word asks the questions, "Who is it you have insulted and blasphemed? Against whom have you raised your voice and lifted your eyes in pride? Against the Holy One of Israel!" (2 Kings 19:22). Please help me to have a proper respect for You, O God. Keep me from disrespecting You by thinking too much—or too little—of myself.

_____

_____

_____

_____

_____

_____

_____

_____

_____

_____

_____

_____

_____

_____

_____

_____

_____

_____

Father, help us possess only acceptable kinds of pride such as taking pride in those who set a good example (2 Corinthians 5:12). Then, even in all our troubles, as we take godly pride in one another, our joy may know no bounds (2 Corinthians 7:4).

A TIME TO BE SILENT

Brothers, if someone is caught in a sin,
you who are spiritual should restore him gently.
But watch yourself, or you also may be tempted.

—Galatians 6:1

There is a big difference between confessing our sins to God and confessing our sins to others, because He can always take it. He can forgive and be trusted not to bring it back up.

Refreshingly, some believers can too. But some of them can't take the gory details without stumbling over them. Therefore, we do not always need to tell others every detail of every sin we've ever committed. The King James Version translates James 5:16 accurately, telling us to confess our "faults" one to another. Note the slight contrast between sharing our *faults* with others and the act of confessing *every detail of every sin* to our brothers and sisters. If we're confessing for the right reasons, we'll take others into account.

There are times to share your heart and times to simply celebrate God's forgiveness.

Father, help me to encourage others daily, as long as it is called "today," so that they may not be hardened by sin's deceitfulness (Hebrews 3:13). In my conversations with others, may I spend less time sharing the details of my sins and more time praising You for Your glorious way of conquering and forgiving them.

_____

_____

_____

_____

_____

_____

_____

_____

_____

_____

_____

_____

_____

_____

_____

_____

_____

_____

Heal me, O Lord, and I will be healed; save me and I will be saved, for You are the one I praise (Jeremiah 17:14). I will speak your name more—and my name less.

PERFECTLY SATISFIED

In righteousness I will see your face;
when I awake, I will be satisfied with seeing your likeness.

— *Psalm 17:15*

I am convinced that our hearts are not healthy until they have been satisfied by the only completely healthy love that exists: the love of God Himself.

The following words by Oswald Chambers are not only written in the front of my Bible; they are engraved deeply in my mind: "No love of the natural heart is safe unless the human heart has been satisfied by God first."

We are not free to love in the true intent of the word until we have found love. All of us have looked, but the important question is *where?* In the search for unfailing love, if we unknowingly allow Satan to become our tour guide, the quest will undoubtedly lead to captivity.

Others' love is often
restricted to good times.
God's love is for all time.

Show me Your ways, O Lord, teach me Your paths; guide me in Your truth and teach me, for You are God my Savior, and my hope is in You all day long. Remember, O Lord, Your great mercy and love, for they are from of old. Remember not the sins of my youth and my rebellious ways; according to Your love remember me, for You are good, O Lord (Psalm 25:4–7).

My Lord, You are the faithful God, keeping Your covenant of love to a thousand generations of those who love You and keep Your commands (Deuteronomy 7:9).

A HISTORY OF REJECTION

Already the Jews had decided that anyone who acknowledged that Jesus was the Christ would be put out of the synagogue.

—John 9:22

Scripture tells us that certain Pharisees who really wanted to believe in Jesus were afraid to express their acceptance of Christ for fear of the rejection and exclusion from their communities. Rejection truly has a long pedigree. We're not the first. We're not the last. But it hurts just the same.

If you've never experienced rejection, you might be wondering whether *suffering* is too strong a word for it; however, if you have been rejected by someone you love, you'll agree that few injuries are more excruciating. Yet although we understand that betrayals and heartaches too often come with the territory of earthly living, our great hope is in a great God whose love is greater than our rejection.

> *The pain of rejection is very widespread, very real. And God is very aware of it.*

Lord God, Your Spirit Himself testifies with our spirit that we are Your children. Now if we are children, then we are heirs—heirs of Yours and coheirs with Christ, if indeed we share in His sufferings in order that we may also share in His glory. Help me embrace the truth that any present sufferings I encounter are not worth comparing with the glory that will be revealed in me (Romans 8:16–18).

Lord, I desire to claim the words Moses delivered to Your ancient people: help me not to be afraid. Enable me to stand firm so I will see the deliverance that You, the Lord, will bring me today. You, Lord, will fight for me; help me only to be still (Exodus 14:13–14).

Not on My Own

For Christ's sake, I delight in weaknesses, in insults, in hardships,
in persecutions, in difficulties. For when I am weak, then I am strong.
—2 Corinthians 12:10

In Your Own Words

God may have used some kind of plan or method to set someone else free that doesn't work as effectively for you. Perhaps the success of others has done little more than increase your own discouragement and self-hatred.

Don't let the enemy play mind games with you. God's strength is tailor-made for weakness. In fact, when we admit our weakness, it draws God like a magnet. We are never stronger than the moment we admit we are weak.

Seek God diligently and ask Him to show you the way to victory. Use Scripture prayers in conjunction with any plan He sets forth for you. But trust *Him*, not a method, to be your strength.

> *Awareness of our weakness*
> *is a sign of great strength.*

My Lord and Creator, I confess to you that I, like everyone else in the human condition, am weak in my natural self. I used to offer the parts of my body in slavery to impurities. I have personally experienced the ever-increasing nature of wickedness. But now I offer my body in slavery to righteousness leading to holiness (Romans 6:19). Thank You, Father, that no matter how I've been enslaved, You can set me free!

O Lord, You hem me in—behind and before; You have laid Your hand upon me. I do not need to feel shame or fear in Your intimate knowledge of my life, because Your Word says that Your knowledge of me is wonderful! (Psalm 139:5-6).

THE FORCE OF HIS WILL

Which things have indeed a show of wisdom in will worship,
and humility, and neglecting of the body; not in any honor to the
satisfying of the flesh. —*Colossians 2:23 (KJV)*

IN YOUR OWN WORDS

The King James Version uses an interesting phrase in this passage: "will worship." You see, if we could truly subdue all our fleshly appetites by the pure power of our determination, we would simply worship our own will.

Paradoxically, we discover liberty through the will of *God*. He will never allow us continued success through our fleshly determination. He knows we would simply end up worshiping our own wills and methods.

It is only through the might of the Holy Spirit released through the authority of His Word that we are empowered to say no to the things we should—and say yes to freedom, moderation, and better health.

Willpower only works up to a point.
God's power works to the end.

Help my soul, Lord, to find rest in You alone; my hope comes from You. You alone are my rock and my salvation; You are my fortress, I will not be shaken. My salvation and my honor depend on You; You, God, are my mighty rock, my refuge. Help me to trust in You at all times. Remind me to pour out my heart to You, for You, God, are my refuge (Psalm 62:5-8).

Lord, according to Your Word, if I wholeheartedly commit whatever I do to You, my plans will succeed (Proverbs 16:3). Lord, I acknowledge that the heart of committing any plan to You is seeking *Your* plan. Show me the right path, Father!

NO REGRETS

Godly sorrow brings repentance that leads to salvation and leaves no regret, but worldly sorrow brings death.

—2 Corinthians 7:10

IN YOUR OWN WORDS

When God opened my eyes to this verse, I wept before the Lord over a particular sin and said, "I want to have godly sorrow so that I can be free . . . but I don't, Lord! What can I do? Am I stuck with it forever?"

His tender response was the same one He's given me virtually every time I have longed for something I lacked: "Pray for it, My child." So I began to pray for godly sorrow to come to me over that cherished sin.

It came at first like the gentle morning tide, but ultimately it hit me like a tidal wave. I did not realize until then how different the concepts of regret and repentance are.

> *Godly sorrow is a change of heart, not a wave of emotion.*

O merciful God, when a prayer or plea is made by any of Your people—each one aware of his afflictions and pains, and spreading out his hands toward You—then hear from heaven, Your dwelling place. Forgive, and deal with me according to all I do, since You know my heart (for You alone know the hearts of men), so that I will fear You and walk in Your ways all the days of my life (2 Chronicles 6:29-31).

Lord, although my sins testify against me, do something for the sake of Your name. For my backsliding is great; I have sinned against You (Jeremiah 14:7).

UP TO HIS OLD TRICKS

To whom ye forgive anything, I forgive also . . . lest Satan should get an advantage of us: for we are not ignorant of his devices.
—2 Corinthians 2:10-11 (KJV)

IN YOUR OWN WORDS

Don't expect Satan to let you off the hook of unforgiveness easily. Be prepared to recommit to forgiveness every day until you're free.

Second Corinthians 2:11 warns us to forgive "lest Satan should get an advantage of us: for we are not ignorant of his devices." The Word of God clearly teaches that Satan takes tremendous advantage of any unforgiveness in our lives. Unforgiveness qualifies as one of the most powerfully effective forms of bondage in any believer's life. Our bodies simply cannot tolerate it.

Yes, this stronghold demands serious demolition, but the liberty you will feel when you finally let go is inexpressible! Forgiveness is the ultimate "weight loss!"

The devil will keep using whatever works on us.

O God, I will not say to a person who has hurt me, "I'll pay you back for this wrong!" I will wait for You, Lord, and You will deliver Me (Proverbs 20:22). I will not say of someone who has wronged me, "I'll do to him as he has done to me; I'll pay that man back for what he did" (Proverbs 24:29). I will not be taken in so easily by the devil's lies.

Lord God, help me to speak and act as those who are going to be judged by the law that gives freedom, because judgment without mercy will be shown to anyone who has not been merciful. Mercy triumphs over judgment! (James 2:12-13).

A Better Way to Fight

God looks down from heaven on the sons of men to see if there are
any who understand, any who seek God.

—Psalm 53:2

Much of the Word applies specifically to the battles we face against Satan. The Bible has much to say about fighting the good fight of faith and becoming well-trained soldiers. But it has far more to say about the pure pursuit of God, His righteousness, and His plan for us.

I believe a wise conclusion to draw from these emphases in the Word of God is this: yes, give much time and thought to becoming well-equipped victors in the battle that rages, but give more time to the pursuit of the heart of God and all things concerning Him.

Much about warfare. More about God Himself. That, my friend, is the way to victory!

> *By ourselves,*
> *we're no match for the devil.*
> *But he is no match for our God.*

Father God, I thank You that those who belong to You were meant to be the head, not the tail! If I am obedient to You, O Lord, and do not turn aside from Your ways, You will not allow the enemy to keep me at the bottom (Deuteronomy 28:13-14).

Reach down from on high, my God, my Redeemer, and take hold of me! Draw me out of deep waters. Rescue me from my powerful enemy, from my foes, who are too strong for me! My enemy has confronted me in the day of my disaster, but You, Lord, are my support (Psalm 18:16-18).

SINISTER SINS

Do you not know that your body is a temple of the Holy Spirit, who is in you, whom you have received from God? You are not your own.

—1 Corinthians 6:19

IN YOUR OWN WORDS

All sin is equal in the sense of eternal ramifications, but not all sin is equal in its earthly impact. Satan knows that sexual sin is unique in its attack and impact on the body of the individual believer.

Since the Spirit of Christ now dwells in the temple of believers' bodies, getting a Christian engaged in sexual sin is the closest Satan can come to personally assaulting Christ. That ought to make us mad enough to be determined to live victoriously! Sins against the body have a strange way of sticking to us, making us feel like we literally *are* that sin rather than being a person who commits it. Sexual sin has a cancerous effect on who we are, how we think, and what we do.

> *Your body is the Lord's house.*
> *Don't junk it up.*

Father, help me, enable me, strengthen me to put to death whatever belongs to my earthly nature: sexual immorality, impurity, lust, evil desires and greed, which is idolatry. Because of these, Your wrath is coming. I used to walk in these ways, in the life I once lived (Colossians 3:5-7). Help me to understand that "putting to death" means to cease empowering it, fueling it, or doing things that arouse it to unholy life.

You, God, created my inmost being; You knit me together in my mother's womb. I praise You because I am fearfully and wonderfully made; Your works are wonderful. I know that full well (Psalm 139:13-14). My body is not horrible. I have simply misused it. Please sanctify it and take it over completely.

YOU AMAZE ME

"I have revealed and saved and proclaimed—I, and not some foreign god among you. You are my witnesses," declares the LORD, "that I am God."

—Isaiah 43:12

IN YOUR OWN WORDS

God warned His people over and over that if they did not resist the false gods of the nations surrounding them, they would be snared and He would ultimately allow them to be taken captive.

They didn't and He did.

One sobering thing about the faithfulness of God is that He keeps His promises, even when they are promises of judgment or discipline.

Over and over the Book of Isaiah seems to plead the question, "Why in the world would you worship idols when you have been chosen by the sovereign God of the universe to be His own?" But aren't we often guilty of the same thing? He has chosen us for His own. Are we choosing to live in daily gratitude?

It doesn't cost nearly so much to serve the Living God as it costs to serve idols.

You, my Lord, are the everlasting God, the Creator of the ends of the earth. You will not grow tired or weary, and Your understanding no one can fathom. You give strength to the weary and increase the power of the weak. Even youths grow tired and weary, and young men stumble and fall; but when I hope in You, Lord, my strength will be renewed. I will soar on wings like eagles; I will run and not grow weary, I will walk and not faint (Isaiah 40:28-31).

O Lord, help me to lift my eyes and look to the heavens and acknowledge who created all these. You bring out the starry host one by one, and call each of them by name. Because of Your great power and mighty strength, not one of them is missing (Isaiah 40:26). What a faithful Father you are!

COMING CLEAN

Jesus replied, "I tell you the truth, everyone who sins is a slave to sin. Now a slave has no permanent place in the family, but a son belongs to it forever. So if the Son sets you free, you will be free indeed."
—*John 8:34-36*

IN YOUR OWN WORDS

If we are going to live in freedom, we have no choice but to renounce every single secret place of sin in our lives to God, exposing even the smallest detail to the light of God's Word. I have also found incalculable help and freedom in confessing details of my past sins and strongholds to a few other trustworthy, mature believers for the sake of accountability.

Living a consistently victorious life takes courage! But this courage leads to glorious, indescribable liberty! What relief awaits you if you really decide to let God's truth set you free . . . and to let His truth continue *keeping* you free. Be willing to ask God on a regular basis if you are overlooking or denying a stronghold in your life.

> *The truth does hurt sometimes. But it ultimately heals us from the inside out.*

Father, Your Word says, "Whoever invokes a blessing in the land will do so by the God of truth; he who takes an oath in the land will swear by the God of truth. For the past troubles will be forgotten and hidden from my eyes" (Isaiah 65:16). Lord, I have plenty of past troubles. They seem to continue to be right before my eyes. Please, God of truth, invoke a blessing over my life and release me from my past.

O God, send forth Your light and Your truth to my life. Let them guide me; let them bring me to Your holy mountain, to the place where You dwell (Psalm 43:3).

HOW GREAT A LOVE

Love never fails. But where there are prophecies, they will cease; where there are tongues, they will be stilled; where there is knowledge, it will pass away.

—1 Corinthians 13:8

We are not wrong to think we desperately need to be loved. We do. But we are wrong to think we can make anyone love us the way we need to be loved. Our need does not constitute anyone else's call but God's.

Many of us have heard the devastating words, "I just don't love you any more." Others may not have heard the words, but they have felt the feeling. Throughout life we will lose people either to death or changing circumstances who really loved us. As dear and as rich as their love was, it was not unending. It moved. It died. It changed. It left wonderful memories . . . but it left a hole. Only God's love never ends, never fails, never dies, never changes.

> *Even the best love is only ours for a season. God's love alone will last forever.*

Jesus Christ, my Kinsman Redeemer and my Bridegroom, Your banner over me is love! (Song of Songs 2:4).

Lord God, help me to trust in Your unfailing love; cause my heart to rejoice in Your salvation. Help me to sing to You, Lord, for You have been good to me! (Psalm 13:5-6).

TODAY AND EVERY DAY

"If serving the LORD seems undesirable to you, then choose for yourselves this day whom you will serve. . . . But as for me and my household, we will serve the LORD."

—*Joshua 24:15*

IN YOUR OWN WORDS

The concept of rededicating our lives to Christ only at infrequent revival services or conferences can prove disappointing and defeating. Joshua suggests a far more workable approach: "Choose for yourselves *this day* whom you will serve."

True, a daily recommitment does not ensure that we'll never fail, but it helps us develop the mentality that every day is a new day, a new chance to follow Christ. Obedience to God is not some diet we suddenly blow and have to wait till Monday to start again. It is something to which we recommit ourselves every day, no matter how we blew it the day before. Victorious living is not an instant arrival but the joy of watching God form victorious habits in us.

Victorious living is the pursuit of one victorious day at a time.

Lord, I know what it is to be in need, and I know what it is to have plenty. I want to learn the secret of being content in any and every situation, whether well fed or hungry, whether living in plenty or in want. I can do everything through You, Lord, who gives me strength (Philippians 4:12-13). But help me remember that I must rely on Your strength the first thing every morning.

O Father, please help me be a doer of Your Word and not a hearer only, deceiving myself (James 1:22). If I am to experience You personally, I must be obedient to You. Starting today. Starting right now.

REAL REPENTANCE

"First to those in Damascus, then to those in Jerusalem and in all Judea, and to the Gentiles also, I preached that they should repent and turn to God and prove their repentance by their deeds."

—*Acts 26:20*

IN YOUR OWN WORDS

When we pray the Scriptures in regard to our sins, it helps ensure the presence of true repentance, and helps us bask in the freedom of forgiveness. If biblical repentance has not taken place, what we are calling "guilt" is probably the active, faithful conviction of the Holy Spirit.

I remember a time in my college years when I was deeply puzzled about ongoing feelings of guilt over a sin for which I had asked forgiveness many times. I could not understand why I never felt out from under the weight or burden of it. But God showed me that I had cherished that sin in my heart, hanging on to it emotionally though I had let go of it physically. Obedience must become our heart's desire.

> *Guilt is a nag,*
> *and only true repentance*
> *can help you put it in its place.*

In tears I have sought You, Lord. I desire to come and bind myself to You in an everlasting covenant that will not be forgotten (Jeremiah 50:4-5). So Father, give me a heart to know You, that You are the Lord. I am Yours and You are mine, for I have returned to You with all my heart (Jeremiah 24:7). You have said that if I will return to You, the Lord Almighty, You will return to me (Malachi 3:7).

_____

_____

_____

_____

_____

_____

_____

_____

_____

_____

_____

_____

_____

_____

_____

_____

_____

See, O Lord, how distressed I am! I am in torment within, and in my heart I am disturbed, for I have been most rebellious (Lamentations 1:20). But thank You, my merciful Father, for the assurance that You will not despise a broken and contrite heart (Psalm 51:17).

TELL GOD ON THEM

Hear me, O God, as I voice my complaint; protect my life from the threat of the enemy.

—Psalm 64:1

If you are unable to forgive a certain individual, an important part of breaking free is learning to pray about and for the person. But there is a difference between praying *about* a person and praying *for* a person, and both kinds of prayer are intended by God to change our own hearts.

Today, let's just look at the first one. My experience has been that praying *about* the person who has hurt us is necessary before we can find any real measure of freedom to sincerely pray *for* the person. *Yes, I'm talking about tattling*—telling God what they've done to you and how upset you are, telling Him all the things you feel and how unfair you believe someone has been to you. God is the one Person big enough to take it!

> *We are invited to bring our complaints to God when we are overwhelmed.*

This is the only segment of the book where I will not be supplying you with certain Scriptures to pray. This kind of prayer necessitates the sharing of your own very personal feelings. I wanted to make sure we addressed the importance of praying *about* someone who has hurt you because it is such a vital part of breaking free. Be honest with God. Pour out your heart to Him. Tell Him the things that hurt you. Tell on the one who injured you. Search the Psalms to receive further permission to speak your heart, then practice it—from your own heart with your own words! *How often and for how long?* you might ask. As often as you need (you'll probably need much more than this page!) . . . and don't stop until all the bitter waters have been poured out before God and He's had a chance to begin pouring living water back in.

PRAYING FOR THE ENEMY

*All of you, live in harmony with one another; be sympathetic, love
as brothers, be compassionate and humble. Do not repay evil with
evil or insult with insult, but with blessing, because to this you were
called so that you may inherit a blessing.*   —1 Peter 3:8~9

IN YOUR OWN WORDS

After we've practiced pouring our hearts out to God through praying *about* a person we're struggling to forgive, it's time to additionally begin praying *for* that person.

I already know what you may be thinking, because I used to feel the same way. *Why should I pray for a person who has hurt me so badly?* But God's ways are not our ways. He created our psyches, and He alone knows how they operate. He created our hearts so uniquely; they are forced to forgive in order to be free.

God greatly honors our willingness to bless others when our human reaction would be to curse them. Today's verse says it all: "to this you were called so that you may inherit a blessing."

*We are called to be free.
Therefore, we are called to forgive.*

Father, I pray that You will love _____ through me with love that is patient and kind. Love that does not envy, does not boast, and is not proud. Love that is not rude and is not self-seeking. Love that is not easily angered and keeps no record of wrongs. Love that does not delight in evil but rejoices with the truth. Love that always protects, always trusts, always hopes, always perseveres (1 Corinthians 13:4-7).

Lord, I pray that wisdom will enter _____'s heart, and knowledge will be pleasant to his soul. I pray that discretion will protect him, understanding will guard him, and that wisdom will save him from the ways of wicked men (Proverbs 2:10–12).

Dear God, I pray that _____ will trust in You wilh all her heart and lean not on her own understanding, that if in all of her ways she acknowledges You, You will make her paths straight. I pray that she would not be wise in her own eyes but would fear You and shun evil, for this will bring health to her body and nourishment to her whole life (Proverbs 3:5-8).

THE TIES THAT BIND

"Haven't you read," [Jesus] replied, "that at the beginning the Creator 'made them male and female,' and said, 'For this reason a man will leave his father and mother and be united to his wife, and the two will become one flesh'?"   —*Matthew 19:4-5*

IN YOUR OWN WORDS

Sexual engagement forms a soul tie that was meant for marriage alone. First Corinthians 6:16 says, "Do you not know that he who unites himself with a prostitute is one with her in body? For it is said, 'The two will become one flesh.' "

When we engage in any realm of sexual intimacy with someone besides our marriage partner, we are tying ourselves to them. It can form a soul tie that is absolutely out of the will of God and must be renounced severely in order for such surrendered ground to be reclaimed.

A soul tie to anyone besides our spouse becomes an open target for the continuing, destroying schemes of the devil.

> *Our spouses are not always everything we wish they'd be. But are we?*

Father God, Your Word says that I have been made holy through the sacrifice of the body of Jesus Christ (Hebrews 10:10). Being holy means that I have been set apart for sacred use rather than common use. If I cleanse myself, I will be an instrument for noble purposes, made holy, useful to the Master and prepared to do any good work (2 Timothy 2:21).

Lord, according to Your Word, a person can be handed over to Satan, so that the sinful nature may be destroyed and his or her spirit saved on the day of the Lord (1 Corinthians 5:5). Help me not to continue resisting repentance and be handed over to Satan for a season. Help me turn my life over to You now.

A CHANGE OF HEART

I cried out to him with my mouth; his praise was on my tongue.
If I had cherished sin in my heart, the Lord would not have listened.
—Psalm 66:17-18

IN YOUR OWN WORDS

Have you ever physically turned from a sin and ceased the activity, yet continued to cherish it to some degree in your heart? Godly sorrow is not defined by tears or outward displays of contrition but by a change of heart resulting in complete agreement with God over the matter.

You may say, *But Beth, I can't change the way I feel.* I understand. I've been there too. But that's why it's called "godly sorrow." Only He can change our hearts, "for God is greater than our hearts, and he knows everything" (1 John 3:19). And that's all He is waiting for us to do: to invite Him to change our hearts and bring about the supernatural work of true repentance. He's looking for our willingness to let go of the sin.

> *Until a heart change comes,*
> *we continue to live at high risk*
> *of sinful actions.*

Lord, who can discern his errors? Forgive my hidden faults. Keep Your servant also from willful sins; may they not rule over me. Then will I be blameless, innocent of great transgression. May the words of my mouth and the meditation of my heart be pleasing in Your sight, O Lord, my Rock and my Redeemer (Psalm 19:12-14).

_____

_____

_____

_____

_____

_____

_____

_____

_____

_____

_____

_____

_____

_____

_____

_____

_____

Lord, I acknowledged my sin to You and did not cover up my iniquity. I said, "I will confess my transgressions to the Lord"—and You forgave the guilt of my sin (Psalm 32:5).

RESURRECTION POWER

My message and my preaching were not with wise and persuasive words, but with a demonstration of the Spirit's power, so that your faith might not rest on men's wisdom, but on God's power.

—1 Corinthians 2:4-5

IN YOUR OWN WORDS

God applies the same power to our need that He exerted when He raised Christ from the dead. I find myself being reminded of that when I come across a difficulty or challenge that seems too big for me, something that seems simply impossible to perform or overcome.

Imagine the power required to resuscitate life into a body that had been dead for three days. Think of the power that trembled throughout the earth at the Lord's crucifixion, when the temple curtain was ripped in two and the tombs of the saints broke open into new life.

Does your stronghold require more power than it takes to raise the dead? Neither does mine! God can do it. He says so. He's done it for me.

> *If we knew the power that worked in us, we'd not be so worked up over our problems.*

Christ Jesus, You spoke boldly to Your disciples with the promise: "If you have faith as small as a mustard seed, you can say to this mountain, 'Move from here to there' and it will move. Nothing will be impossible for you" (Matthew 17:20). Lord, develop in me the kind of faith that moves mountains in the power of Your Spirit.

Lord, I pray that out of Your glorious riches You may strengthen me with power through Your Spirit in my inner being, so that You, Lord Jesus, may dwell in my heart through faith (Ephesians 3:16-17).

THE END OF PRIDE

He has brought down rulers from their thrones
but has lifted up the humble.

—Luke 1:52

IN YOUR OWN WORDS

Pride is the welcome mat in every figurative prison cell. All we have to do to remain bound in any area is to refuse to do two things: to take responsibility for our strongholds and to repent of the sin involved. And pride is what keeps us from doing both.

So I'd like to brag on you a moment. You wouldn't be holding this book in your hands if you didn't have enough humility to admit to the threat of a stronghold or two. You're wise enough to know that you probably need to pray a few Scriptures every day that confront your pride. We never waste our time when we pray about our tendency toward pride and seek to humble ourselves before God.

When we hold on to pride,
we miss so many things
God has for us.

Father, You led Your children, the Israelites, all the way in the desert for forty years, to humble them in order to know what was in their hearts, whether or not they would keep Your commands (Deuteronomy 8:2). Help me understand that sometimes You lead me on certain paths to humble me, to see what is in my heart. Purify my heart, Lord, so that You will take joy in what You find.

God, Your Word clearly warns us that pride goes before destruction, a haughty spirit before a fall (Proverbs 16:18). I desire to stand with You, Lord—to make You my pride and joy.

THE WAY OF TRUTH

Whether you turn to the right or to the left, your ears will hear a voice behind you, saying, "This is the way; walk in it."

—Isaiah 30:21

IN YOUR OWN WORDS

Because of my past track record, I've had to learn to dialogue openly with God about areas of my life that are at risk: areas where I've been defeated before or circumstances that suddenly result in anger or insecurity. I also ask Him to help me discern the very first signs of Satan's deceptions in my life.

The most effective way to veer from deception is to walk in truth. Third John 4 says, "I have no greater joy than to hear that my children are walking in the truth." The joy that results from your walk in truth won't just be God's. It will be yours too. As Christ said, "I have told you this so that my joy may be in you and that your joy may be complete" (John 15:11).

Let truth have its way in your life, and joy won't be far behind.

My all-powerful God, enable me to stand firm, with the belt of truth buckled around my waist and with the breastplate of righteousness in place (Ephesians 6:14). Help me to understand that without the girding of truth, I am defenseless against the devil and set up for failure. Truth is my main defense against the father of lies.

Test me, O Lord, and try me, examine my heart and my mind; for Your love is ever before me, and I desire to walk continually in Your truth (Psalm 26:2–3).

YOUR MORNING CUP

Let the morning bring me word of your unfailing love, for I have put my trust in you. Show me the way I should go, for to you I lift up my soul.

—Psalm 143:8

We each have our unmet needs, and we carry them around all day long like an empty cup. In one way or another, we hold out that empty cup to the people in our lives and say, *"Can somebody please fill this? Even a tablespoon would help!"*

Whether we seek to have our cup filled through approval, affirmation, control, success, or immediate gratification, we are miserable until something is in it. What a heavy yoke is shattered when we awaken in the morning, bring our hearts, minds, and souls and all their needs to God, offer Him our empty cups, and ask Him to fill them with Himself! No one is more pleasurable to be around than a person who has had her cup filled by the Lord Jesus Christ.

Where have you brought your empty cup today? How is it being filled?

Father God, Your Word says for everyone who is godly to pray to You while You may be found. What an honor to be counted among that number! Surely when the mighty waters rise, they will not reach me. You are my hiding place; You will protect me from trouble and surround me with songs of deliverance (Psalm 32:6-7).

God of all grace, I have the assurance of Your Word that, after I have suffered a little while, You who called me to Your eternal glory in Christ Jesus will restore me and make me strong, firm, and steadfast (1 Peter 5:10).

Your Daddy's Delight

"I give them eternal life, and they shall never perish; no one can snatch them out of my hand."

—John 10:28

In Your Own Words

No matter what rejection you may face in life, remember God will not reject you. His Word says, "God did not reject his people, whom he foreknew" (Romans 11:2). Even when He must discipline you, He does so in absolute love.

God was pleased to make you His own. He didn't just feel sorry for you. He wasn't obligated to you. He chose you because He delights in you. You were never meant to get through life by the skin of your teeth. You were meant to flourish in the love and acceptance of Almighty Jehovah.

"He will take great delight in you, he will quiet you with his love, he will rejoice over you with singing" (Zephaniah 3:17).

You are the apple of your Father's eye, the joy of your Father's heart.

Lord God, just as Your children the Israelites were chosen out of all the peoples on the face of the earth to be Your people, Your treasured possession, I believe that we, the body of Christ, have been chosen too. You did not set Your affection on Your children and choose us because we were more numerous than other peoples. It was because You loved us that You redeemed us from slavery, from the power of the enemy (Deuteronomy 7:6-8).

_____

_____

_____

_____

_____

_____

_____

_____

_____

_____

_____

_____

_____

_____

_____

_____

Jesus, teach me not to let my heart be troubled. In Your Father's house are many rooms, and You have gone there to prepare a place for me. You will most assuredly come back and take me to be with You some day so that I may also be where You are (John 14:1-3).

THE CHOICE TO LIVE

Those controlled by the sinful nature cannot please God.
You, however, are controlled not by the sinful nature
but by the Spirit, if the Spirit of God lives in you.

—Romans 8:8-9

IN YOUR OWN WORDS

Some of the people I respect most are those who have allowed God to set them free from the strangling stronghold of addiction. I pray that if you suffer from some form of addiction—or love someone who does—God will use Scripture prayers dramatically in your life, in their lives.

May He enable you, His servant, to speak His Word "with great boldness," and may He stretch out His hand to heal and perform miraculous signs and wonders through the name of His holy servant, Jesus (Acts 4:29–30).

Be tenacious and patient, child of God. If you fall, don't listen to the accusations and jeers of the evil one. Get back up and walk with God again. How many times? Until you're free.

In God alone,
there is lasting freedom.

My merciful God, I have learned the hard way that nothing good lives in me, that is, in my sinful nature. For I have the desire to do what is good, but I cannot carry it out (Romans 7:18). But in You I have the power I need! You've given me the treasure of the Holy Spirit who lives in this weak jar of clay to show that this all-surpassing power is from You and not from me! (2 Corinthians 4:7).

Father, I claim Your Word that says I did not receive a spirit that makes me a slave again to fear, but I received the Spirit of sonship. And by Him I cry, "Abba, Father" (Romans 8:15).

I GIVE UP

God did not give us a spirit of timidity,
but a spirit of power, of love and of self-discipline.

—2 Timothy 1:7

IN YOUR OWN WORDS

So, are you just about to give up? Good—as long as you're giving yourself up to God, to the authority of His Holy Spirit. Both Galatians 5:22 and 2 Timothy 1:7 tell us that self-discipline is a work of the Spirit. So stop feeling guilty because you don't have any self-discipline on your own. Neither does that together-looking person next to you. None of us can master ourselves. God is the only One who can sanctify and make every part of us whole.

All He wants is our trust, our belief, and a little time. You never have to wonder if God's will includes you being liberated from your strongholds. The answer is yes, so begin praying His will over your life with confidence.

When you realize you have no fight left,
God has you right where He wants you.

O God, You are my God, earnestly I seek You; my soul thirsts for You, my body longs for You, in a dry and weary land where there is no water. I have seen You in the sanctuary and beheld Your power and Your glory. Because Your love is better than life, my lips will glorify You. I will praise You as long as I live, and in Your name I will lift up my hands (Psalm 63:1-4).

Lord, continue to teach me with regard to my former way of life, to put off my old self (Ephesians 4:22) and to put on the new self, created to be like You, God, in true righteousness and holiness (Ephesians 4:24).

JUDGE AND JURY

Who will bring any charge against those whom God has chosen?
It is God who justifies.

—*Romans 8:33*

IN YOUR OWN WORDS

Once true repentance has taken place, any accusation and guilt we continue to feel are from the enemy. In the life of a believer, guilt experienced *before* repentance is the conviction of the Holy Spirit. Guilt experienced *after* repentance is the condemnation of the evil one.

So if you have truly repented of sin, you are forgiven no matter how you happen to feel. I finally realized in my own life that when I was unwilling to accept Christ's complete forgiveness after I had genuinely repented, my problem was an authority problem. I was in effect saying Christ couldn't do His job. And I found myself having to repent for refusing to receive forgiveness! Sin given to God is gone forever.

True repentance leaves behind no remains.

Lord, Your Word says that if Your people will turn now, each of us, from our evil practices, we can stay in the land You have given us (Jeremiah 25:5). Lord, You have heard my plea for mercy; You, the Lord, will accept my prayer (Psalm 6:9).

_____

_____

_____

_____

_____

_____

_____

_____

_____

_____

_____

_____

_____

_____

_____

_____

_____

_____

_____

Father, thank You for disciplining me for my good, that I may share in Your holiness (Hebrews 12:10). And thank You for assuring me in Your Word that the ones You rebuke and discipline are those You love (Revelation 3:19).

FIGHTING WORDS

"The LORD your God, who is going before you, will fight for you, as he did for you in Egypt, before your very eyes."

—*Deuteronomy 1:30*

Satan is an opportunist. Would he come after you while you are down? In a heartbeat (if he *had* a heart). The word *appropriate* isn't in his vocabulary. He's not polite; he fights dirty; he doesn't give us room to wait until we're on our feet again so we can have a fair fight.

I know that most of us would rather not have to think about warfare when we are hurting, when we are grieving a death, when we are suffering a wrong, but—somehow, some way—we must muster the energy to take protective measures. Pray for protection through your season of grief. Call on intercessors to pray for you. Keep talking to God, and believe His Word that tells us He can and will restore abundant life.

When you can't fight back, remember that God does the fighting for you.

I love You, Lord, for You heard my voice; You heard my cry for mercy. Because You turned Your ear to me, I will call on You as long as I live. The cords of death entangled me, the anguish of the grave came upon me; I was overcome by trouble and sorrow. Then I called to You: "O Lord, save me!" And I found You gracious and righteous; You are full of compassion (Psalm 116:1-5).

Lord, though I walk in the midst of trouble, You preserve my life; You stretch out Your hand against the anger of my foes, with Your right hand You save me. You, Lord, will fulfill Your purpose for me; Your love, O Lord, endures forever—do not abandon the works of Your hands (Psalm 138:7-8).

OPEN UP AND POUR

Trust in him at all times, O people; pour out your hearts to him, for God is our refuge.

—*Psalm 62:8*

Today's verse is not qualified by a disclaimer that says, "Pour out your heart to God if what's inside is nice and sweet." The concept of *pouring out* suggests that some of the contents in our hearts need to go—like hurt, anger, despair, doubt, bitterness, unforgiveness, and confusion. The idea is to pour out the bitter waters that well up in our hearts so that God can pour well-springs of living, sweet waters back in.

When we leave God out of our feelings and emotions, when we don't turn to Him during our temptations and difficult situations, we ignore the fact that He is able and available to treat them! God desires our whole hearts . . . whatever they encase.

Having our hearts cleansed requires emptying them regularly.

Father, my tears have been my food day and night, while men say to me all day long, "Where is your God?" These things I remember as I pour out my soul: how I used to go with the multitude, leading the procession to the house of God, with shouts of joy and thanksgiving among the festive throng (Psalm 42:3-4). Even in times that are much less happy, may I still come and find joy in Your presence.

_____

_____

_____

_____

_____

_____

_____

_____

_____

_____

_____

_____

_____

_____

_____

_____

_____

Lord God, thank You for patiently hearing us when we arise and cry out in the night, as the watches of the night begin, pouring out our hearts like water in Your presence and lifting our hands to You (Lamentations 2:19).

GETTING PAST YOUR PAST

Do not be anxious about anything, but in everything, by prayer and petition, with thanksgiving, present your requests to God.
— *Philippians 4:6*

Is there any hope of earthly recovery from sexual sin, or are we doomed to be defeated by the excess baggage and emptiness that wrong relationships left behind?

The believer in Christ always has hope, but God calls us to some radical responses in order to receive restoration: we must repent wholeheartedly, receive the Lord's loving discipline, and cooperate fully with His plan for recovery. The process can be hard, painful, and somewhat lengthy, because we have to allow God to remove all the broken remnants of the ungodly relationship, to fill in the holes with His loving Spirit until we are smooth and whole. But no matter how hard, the resulting freedom will be worth it.

> *God offers you a clean slate, a straight path, a pure heart.*

Lord, I admit that I reaped absolutely no benefit from the things I am now ashamed of. Those things result in death. But now that I have been set free, the benefit I am reaping leads to holiness, and the result is eternal life. For the wages of sin is death, but Your gift is eternal life in Christ Jesus my Lord (Romans 6:21-23).

Father, I know I can keep my way pure by living according to Your Word. I will seek You with all my heart; help me not to stray from Your commands. Help me to hide Your Word in my heart that I might not sin against You (Psalm 119:9-11).

MOVE TOWARD THE LIGHT

This is the message we have heard from him and declare to you:
God is light; in him there is no darkness at all.

—1 John 1:5

IN YOUR OWN WORDS

Depression becomes a stronghold because its very nature is to eclipse a sense of well-being and hopefulness, strangling our experience of abundant life. And no matter what situation in life causes depression to start, Satan will always take advantage of it.

I believe depression is one of his specialties, because his fingerprints are all over it. Ask ten people to describe their depression in one word, and overwhelmingly the common response will be "darkness." Satan is undoubtedly the prince of darkness—the antithesis of our God, in whom is no darkness at all. The devil can masquerade as an angel of light, but we know where he comes from. We know his true colors.

Satan wants us locked in darkness, but we are assured of his defeat.

God, I feel as though You have put me in the lowest pit, in the darkest depths. Your wrath lies heavily upon me; You have overwhelmed me with all Your waves. You have taken from me my closest friends and have made me repulsive to them. I am confined and cannot escape; my eyes are dim with grief. I call to You, O Lord, every day; I spread out my hands to You (Psalm 88:6-9). Hear my plea!

You, O Lord, keep my lamp burning; You turn my darkness into light. With Your help I can advance against a troop; with You I can scale a wall (Psalm 18:28-29).

HALLELUJAH, WE WIN!

You, dear children, are from God and have overcome them, because the one who is in you is greater than the one who is in the world.

—1 John 4:4

God required a time of deep brokenness in my life before He created in me a healthy heart with the humility and compassion of a true servant. I have a long way to go, but I have put the devil on alert: he may make my life very difficult, but he cannot make me quit. For I, like you, am one of God's dear children, and I have overcome the spirits of darkness only because the One who is in me is greater than the one who is in the world.

What is my revenge after all the devil has done to me? To let God make me twice the foe of hell I would ever have been otherwise. What is my joy? To walk in truth, so aware of the person I have been that I cleave to Christ Jesus like a sash around His priestly robe.

You can walk radically, joyfully, and abundantly in the truth of God's Word.

Father, Your Word tells me that the accuser of believers is overcome by the blood of the Lamb and by the word of our testimony—by those who do not love their lives so much as to shrink from death (Revelation 12:11). Help me to use the power You have given me to overcome the enemy when he wars against me, to stand confidently with You, my Lord and King.

_____

_____

_____

_____

_____

_____

_____

_____

_____

_____

_____

_____

_____

_____

_____

_____

_____

_____

_____

Lord, I pray that You will cause no weapon forged against me to prevail. Enable me to refute the tongue of my accuser. Thank You for giving this as a heritage to Your servants (Isaiah 54:17). Praise Your holy name, O Lord Most High!

SUBJECT INDEX

SCRIPTURE INDEX

Scripture Index

SCRIPTURE INDEX

Scripture Index

IF YOU ENJOYED THIS BOOK
TRY THESE OTHER BETH MOORE TITLES

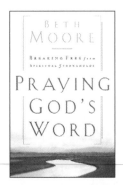

Praying God's Word

0-8054-2351-6

A Heart Like His Devotional Journal

0-8054-3528-X

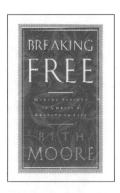

Breaking Free

0-8054-2294-3

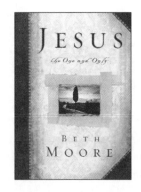

Jesus, The One and Only

0-8054-2489-X